The Church

A Clarion Call to the Body of Christ

Sue Foster

Nation of Women
PUBLISHING

All Scriptures referenced are taken from the Holy Bible, **King James Translation**, 1987 Printing on Bible Gateway. Permission not necessary, Public Domain in the United States.

"The Church Essential"
ISBN # 978-1-7367453-0-4

© 2021 Sue Foster. All rights reserved.
Published by Nation of Women Publishing, Fort Worth, Texas 76114

Printed in United States of America. All rights reserved under International Copyright Law.

No part of this book may be reproduced or transmitted in any form or by any means, electronic or mechanical, including photocopying, recording, or by any information storage or retrieval system, without the express written permission of the publisher.

Table of Contents

Dedication — 5

Introduction — 7

Chapter 1
The Church's Finest Hour — 14
    Maintaining the Proper Perspective
    Essential Components for the Church
    The Church IS Essential

Chapter 2
Two Opposing Agendas — 31
    Discernment
    The Assault on the Church

Chapter 3
Our Responsibility — 41
    The Responsibility of the Five-Fold Ministry
    The Responsibility of Every Believer

Chapter 4
Back to Basics — 58
    Our Fundamental Basics/Essentials

Chapter 5
The Winning Attitude — 70

Receive Jesus as Savior — 80
The Baptism of the Holy Spirit — 81
About the Author — 82

"... Occupy till I come." - Jesus
Luke 19:13

Dedication

It is with much love and appreciation I dedicate "The Church Essential" to our pastor, Dr Bill Winston.

Pastor, thank you for consistently teaching and preaching the uncompromised Word of God. You have equipped me to occupy until Jesus comes and possess lands far beyond what I could have imagined.

I am eternally grateful for your influence in my life.

The Church Essential

Introduction

Essential: *Crucial to the existence, continuance and success of a thing; life-sustaining, vital, fundamental, non-negotiable. An essential component undeniably facilitates the necessary order, structure and alignment required for maximum functionality, performance, endurance and service of a thing.*

We are living in the most remarkable time in the history of mankind. It is the Church's finest hour. I qualify that statement with this Scripture: Habakkuk 2:14 is about to be witnessed by all humanity. What a glorious honor it is to be the generation that disrupts and holds back the forces of evil that have been unleashed as the sands of time quickly run out. God has chosen us for such a time as this to boldly confront every form of darkness, dismantle it, and establish The Kingdom of God everywhere we go.

The devil knows his time to steal, kill, and destroy is extremely short. Hell has been unleashed on planet earth like never before to accomplish satan's agenda specifically crafted for the end times. We are living in a day where there is a ferocious clashing of good versus evil. Yet, many

Christians are unaware of the critical time we are living in, going about their daily lives, oblivious to spiritual realities that are shaping what we see happening right before our eyes.

Tragically, there is a gross lack of discernment amongst Believers; those in ministry and lay people included. A multitude of brothers and sisters who profess Jesus as Savior and Lord are not recognizing the signs of the times, even when hit smack in the face with them on a daily basis. Fake news sources are at work 24/7 to circulate false narratives and propaganda with the intent to pervert the masses' perception of reality; twisting and turning the truth to accommodate the enemy's agenda. Tech giants and social media's mission is luminous; censor, silence, and defame conservative voices that are raising up a standard that indisputably contradict that which evil endeavors to advocate.

There are Spirit-filled Believers who have either chosen to ignore the chaos, anarchy, hate, and division our nation is experiencing, or wrongfully assume, 'this too, shall pass.' Multitudes fail to perceive what part, if any, they have to play in this end time scenario, or they are ill-equipped for what continues to unfold at an accelerated pace. Many Believers are oblivious to where we are in God's prophetic scheme of things, and lives are being destroyed because they lack or have rejected knowledge.

The Church has been deemed unessential, unnecessary, and without value by far-left governing authorities at every level; those who are under the influence of something other than the Holy Spirit. These unrighteous rulers are working a coordinated effort designed and controlled by satan to establish the One World Order, and know it is imperative to shut down and silence the Body of Christ for them to accomplish this objective. At the time of this writing, most of the nation is unable to hold church services per usual, allowed only to hold gatherings with a ludicrous capacity mandated. The mantra of social distancing prohibits the laying on of hands for ministry in many places. Ungodly restrictions are intentionally making it next to impossible for the Church to be the Church, which accentuates the fraudulent label of *unessential* in the eyes of the deceived.

It's one thing for the Church, the Body of Christ, to be considered unessential or irrelevant by those who are cooperating and under the influence of an antichrist spirit. We are not a necessary component, vital to the existence or advancement of their wickedness. In truth, we are a threat to the plans and purposes hell has deemed essential for this hour.

Understand, this is a spiritual battle. Demonic forces are working extremely hard to stop any operation or advancement on our part. But, when we've been labeled as unessential by the casual observer, the lost, or/and our communities, this is no fault but our own. We have failed to operate at our full potential in establishing God's Kingdom on planet earth. Yet, we are more than able to provide innumerable excuses for our lack of productivity upon request. As a result, we're fighting to regain freedoms we once took for granted. Our constitutional rights are in grave jeopardy. Pastors and congregations across the nation are threatened with jail time and outrageous fines for doing what God has instructed the Church to do. We have remained silent and have lacked a higher degree of effectiveness for too long in every realm of society. But God is awakening His Body and preparing us for the greatest move of God which is about to be unleashed across the globe. This is indeed our finest hour.

The purpose of this book is to help the Body of Christ wake up and realize what a critical time we are living in and fulfill the distinguished role we were each born to achieve, as well as what the enemy's agenda is and not be caught unaware when faced with decisions that could potentially cost someone an eternity without Christ. As a child of God, can you think of any greater placement in the history of all mankind, but to be the generation that will help wrap this thing up. Realize, God has saved His best for last, and that's us, Church. It's time for the Body to wake up and get with the program. We have a monumental task at hand, and it requires all hands on deck.

This book is also a clarion call to the five-fold ministry and to anyone in a leadership position in the Church. It is our responsibility to equip, prepare, and mobilize people for what is coming so they in turn can equip, prepare, and mobilize others. We need to thoroughly train all members of the Body of Christ to do the work of the ministry. Our objective is not just to survive but thrive and be productive participants in the work that is yet to be done in advancing the Kingdom of God. This is how God sees us and that is what He says about us.

This is not a time for weak, malnourishing messages. Nor is this the hour for anemic preaching, void of the anointing or the power of the Blood of Jesus. Our fundamental basics are needed now more than ever. Reinforce the Word of God as the final authority in every situation versus religious doctrine, dead religion, or any other comfort zone. Teach on the power in the Name and Blood of Jesus, and how to strategically, intentionally, and skillfully use faith as a surgeon uses a scalpel to achieve desired results.

Put prayer on the front burner. Equip Christ's end-time army with messages that will breed revelation knowledge and teach on the power of our words. Educate on the Baptism of the Holy Spirit, His gifts and how they are needed to do the miraculous. Instruct Believers on the authority that has been delegated to them and how to use this authority as Christ intended. Allow the anointing of the Holy Ghost to destroy yokes and remove bondages in services, Bible studies, and in the marketplace. Train every Believer on what signs should be following them and that the Great Commission is paramount in the life of everyone who calls themselves a Christian. Reinforce the truth that the supernatural is to be normal to every member of the Body of Christ on a daily basis.

God's agenda is for earth to be filled with the knowledge of His glory as the waters cover the sea, according to Habakkuk 2:14, and He is going to use His Body to accomplish this. All creation, the entire earth is waiting for the manifestation of the sons of God; for us to display who our God is, how much

He loves people and hates injustice, no matter what form it comes in. Our families, neighborhoods, cities, states, and nations are waiting on us to demonstrate His Word, that it is not merely religious jargon that is incapable of producing any supernatural evidence that Jesus is alive. It's time for us to show up and be what we're purposed to be by our wonderful God and occupy until Jesus returns. This is our finest hour! Christ in each one of us, in every part of His Body, the indisputable hope of GLORY.

We are the Church and we are essential!

Chapter One

The Church's Finest Hour

This is indeed the Church's finest hour. As the Body of Christ, we are at a pivotal juncture in the history of mankind. This planet is about to be the recipient of a manifestation of this prophetic declaration spoken by the prophet Habakkuk, estimated to be decreed 610 years before Christ. Habakkuk 2:14 says, *"The earth shall be filled with the knowledge of the glory of the Lord as the waters cover the sea,"* and this prophetic agenda of God's cannot be stopped by man nor devil.

The entire planet will be influenced by this end time manifestation of God's glory as the Supernatural Church co-labors with the Holy Spirit, boldly confronting and confounding every type of darkness the enemy unleashes, producing solutions that only the Kingdom of God can supply.

Realize that you have been hand-picked and chosen by God Himself to be an essential part in this end time agenda, anointed for such a time as this to arise and shine as we see the darkness covering the earth (John 15:16, Ephesians 1:4-5). This is the most opportune time in all of history for us to show the world who our God is, starting at home and going forth from there. Multitudes will be led to Christ as a result. Souls! This is our primary objective. Rescue the perishing (Proverbs 11:30, Luke 14:23, 19:10, 2 Timothy 4:2). This end time glory explosion will not only be a time of great miracles like no other, but souls coming into the Kingdom at an exponential rate. We've been created specifically for this end time move of God. We were created for this.

What a tremendous honor and responsibility we have as His Body, each member having a strategic assignment and responsibility in this end time hour. It's time to prepare and position ourselves for what is about to be unleashed by God, as the Holy Spirit directs us. None of us have time to slack off, because we are running out of time. God is about to wrap this thing up. Isaiah 60:1-3 says, *"Arise, shine; for thy light is come, and the glory of the Lord is risen upon thee. For, behold, the darkness shall cover the earth, and gross darkness the people; but the Lord shall arise upon thee, and his glory shall be seen upon thee. And the Gentiles shall come to thy light, and kings to the brightness of thy rising."* God is awakening His Body, the sleeping giant, and the Church of

Jesus Christ is about to occupy planet earth as never before. There is no way hell can stop what God has ordained for this hour (Matthew 16:18).

The Church has been anointed for this hour to rise and shine as hell tries to take over the earth and utterly destroy that which God loves. People. Up to now, the evil has had a much louder voice and a seemingly greater influence and affect than the Body of Christ. This is evident in the seven pillars of influence that impact society: Media, government, education, arts and entertainment, business, church, and the family. We're about to experience a shift that will change the trajectory of what we're witnessing. The enemy has come in like a flood with a 'steal, kill, and destroy' agenda because he knows his time is quickly running out. But our God is raising up His Kingdom standard against satan and his end time agenda (Isaiah 59:19). Our God is placing His people in each pillar of influence to do just that.

We've been called and equipped to infiltrate culture with the light and life of God (Matthew 5:14-16). Evil will be replaced with the good and glorious. There will be a transfer of domination from those cooperating with the enemy to the people of God. The Holy Spirit will do this. The Church is awakening, arising, and disrupting the plans of the kingdom of darkness with Kingdom of God definitives that are impenetrable, indestructible, and uncompromising; and an eternal righteous standard that no foe can thwart and every area of society will be a recipient of the power of the anointing of God.

This is our finest hour, no matter what our five physical senses perceive or try to convince us of. Refuse to be intimidated. Reject the spirit of fear. This is no time to cower, hide, remain passive, or silent. Any anxiety will impair your ability to hear what the Spirit of God is speaking to you. This prophetic agenda from Heaven will bulldoze over the unleashed forces of hell standing in its way. Keep focused. You are a vital part of this chosen generation; exclusively called by God for such a time and task as this. God's people, the ones that truly know Him, will do great exploits in the Name of Jesus (Daniel 11:32), which is bringing glory to God. The anointing will do what it does; destroy yokes and remove burdens (Isaiah 10:27). Miracles, signs, and wonders will follow us that believe the Word in our heart and act on the Word (Mark 16:15-20). As a result, the world will witness and experience undeniable evidence that Jesus is alive!

We must all take this appointment with our destiny seriously. Being key players in this end time scenario is no menial calling. The local church has the potential to impact the globe with the tangible presence and power of God. The miraculous will be the norm for those who know their God and are not ashamed of the Gospel of Jesus Christ. Families, neighborhoods, and local communities will be filled with the experiential knowledge of His glory. Our assignment is clear. Occupy until Jesus comes (Luke 19:13). This is a direct mandate from Christ Himself. Preach and demonstrate the Kingdom of God (1 Corinthians 2:4). It's time to maximize our influence as Kingdom ambassadors over every work of the devil that we encounter and it's going to be by the Spirit of God who dwells in us. Jesus taught His disciples how to pray in Matthew 6. In verse 10, He said, *"Thy kingdom come. Thy will be done in earth, as it is in heaven."* This must be our battle cry, our standard, and agenda. Be determined in your heart to settle for nothing less than this.

Maintaining the Proper Perspective

For the Body of Christ to be the essential and influential force we are created to be, we must remain cognizant of *Whose* we are, *who* we are, and Who is *in* us. We are children of the Most High God, the Great I AM. We belong to Him and we are His beloved, bought by The Blood of Jesus (Ephesians 1:3-6). We're also mighty men and women of God, armed and dangerous in the spirit. The spiritual armor and arsenal we possess, hell cannot even come close to matching. We have Christ in us; The Anointed One and His anointing. The hope of all glory (Colossians 1:27).

It is imperative we understand, as a child of God and joint heir with Jesus, we are seated at the right hand of God the Father because we are in Christ. Ephesians chapters one and two tell us that this position is *far* above any principality, power of darkness, or any name that could be named. This is not about taking a lateral look at circumstances or situations, but having an eternal as Heaven sees it, perspective. Our vantage point from this angle causes us to see and call things as God does, instead of filtering and defining current events based on the information our five physical senses give us. In other words, what does the Word of God say in any given situation versus human logic and reasoning? That is the proper perspective to maintain to help ensure a victorious end to any challenging situation. Refusing to see ourselves as only functioning in a realm limited by natural dictates and directives is a choice we make. Tell the enemy to shut up when he tries to convince you of anything that is contrary to the truth that you are seated with Christ at the right hand of God the Father (Ephesians 2:6). This should be your perspective on anything that would attempt to exalts itself against the knowledge of Christ or try to defy and mock the Word.

The Word of God tells us that we have the solution to every problem, situation, and circumstance that the enemy could coordinate. That solution has a name. His Name is Jesus, Yeshua, Messiah the Anointed One (Luke 1:37, 4:18, Ephesians 1:20-23). The King of Kings and Lord of Lords (Revelation 17:14). It makes no difference as to what type and at what scale the evil has been unleashed against humanity. It doesn't intimidate Heaven, and we must not to allow it to alarm or shake us. The proper perspective is to view and filter everything through the finished works of Jesus. This is our starting place and finish line. Also, as an act of your will, cooperate with the Holy Spirit as He leads. This is a unique time in the history of mankind so we cannot afford to rely on any antiquated ways of thinking, speaking, acting, or (un)believing. All unbelief must be dealt with.

Comfort zones will be challenged. Get used to it and welcome the challenge.

Expect to receive new ideas and strategies in this hour from the Holy Spirit; ideas that may sound unreasonable to your natural mind. Continuing to do business as usual could cause us to miss what God wants to do in us, through us, and for us in this final hour. The status quo, the comfort zones, and the old wineskins must be replaced with the fresh, pliable, and compliant. Humility and our total dependency on Christ are required at all times. We must repent when prompted by the Counselor to do so. It's up to us to be willing to do that complete turnaround, change of mind that will bring us into congruence with the Word and plan of God. Be instantaneous to obey, quick to forgive, and always remain teachable.

This monumental task at hand of disrupting hell's end time agenda is not for the faint of heart. Things are heating up rapidly. Persecution is a guarantee (Matthew 10:22, 2 Timothy 3:12). It takes a Holy Ghost boldness, courage, and resolve to face hell like it needs to be faced – head on. Occasions to exercise our authority and faith are multiplying quickly. The devil is using people in every position and in all walks of life to perpetuate his devastation and destruction in people's lives, property, and future. Deceived, rebellious individuals, and extremely corrupt, demonically energized organizations are calling evil good and good evil, polluting society with these toxins by making them palatable to the hearer (Isaiah 5:20, John 8:44, 1 Timothy 4:1, 2 Timothy 3:13).

A leviathan spirit is using mainstream media to twist and turn truths to the point where the truth is unrecognizable, propagating lies, and programming masses of people to see all areas of life through the veil of gross darkness and deception. An antichrist spirit is stoking the fires of lawlessness, anarchy, violence, hate, and division. Social media platforms are silencing and censoring conservative voices at a rate that was incomprehensible just a short time ago. These platforms are working hard to defame those who raise up a godly standard against that which violates the will of God. But just as the enemy uses people in every position and in all walks of life to perpetuate his evil, God takes people from every position and walk of life, fills them with His Spirit and anoints them to advance His Kingdom across the globe. He qualified each one of us for this time and purpose. Always keep that reality fresh in your mind. You are here now to be that anointed influence.

The United States of America's First Amendment liberties are in critical jeopardy. Our freedom of religion, freedom of speech, and freedom to assemble have a chokehold on them right now. We see a double standard for those who oppose our righteous cause as they turn a blind eye towards the intentionally created chaos in the name of their antichrist mission. Energized and controlled by the demonic, these people are held captive by the darkness and need Jesus (John 8:44). This poses innumerable opportunities for us to continue to stand for that which is right and walk in love simultaneously, no matter how resistant our flesh is to doing just that.

Persecution of those who defy the evil and stand up for our constitutional rights is in our face and meant to silence us. Pastors and their congregations are threatened, fined, and imprisoned for opening church doors enabling people to gather and worship. Church buildings are in danger of being torn down in various cities across the nation by far-left radical politicians that hate God and are under the influence of something other than the Holy Spirit. Peaceful protests are labeled as riotous and unacceptable because they go against the narrative of those who perpetuate corruption and call destructive, dangerous, preplanned, and funded riots, mostly peaceful. Multiple politicians, at every level, are working in tandem with an antichrist spirit to silence the Body of Christ because we are the only ones who can disrupt the plans of satan.

The awakened Church of Jesus Christ is the only authority on earth that can hold back the enemy's agenda to establish the One World Order and usher in the antichrist in this hour (Luke 10:19). We are here to disrupt the plans of hell and establish the government of the Kingdom of God (Matthew 6:10). This is a battle that must be waged in the spirit realm first, cutting evil off at the root, so we can successfully bring into submission everything that is out of Kingdom order and alignment. We are working with the heavenly hosts, an angelic army dispatched by God. There are more with us than against us. We are unstoppable and unconquerable if we maintain our stance and refuse to quit. We are making preparations for the return of our Savior and Lord, Jesus Christ.

Meditating on Scriptures that tell us Whose we are, who we are, and Who lives in us will help us maintain the proper perspective (Joshua 1:8, Psalm 119:97). Our attitude and point of view must be that of Heaven's. Revelation knowledge is required to see these Scriptural realities and be fully persuaded of them. This supernatural insight ignites faith. The only way we walk this assignment out successfully is to live by faith, and we must be determined to do so now more than ever.

When considering the horrendous crisis going on in America, the evil blatantly displayed on our home turf, we must see with the eyes of faith. Remain fixed and focused on the end instead of the beginning, just like our Father God. Say what the Word says (Proverbs 18:21). Refuse to speak words that agree with the lies of the enemy. Put a 24/7 guard over your ear and eye gates. Be mindful what you watch and who you listen to. Keep your thoughts and imaginations on God, and He will keep you in great peace. This peace is supernatural. It defies any natural reasoning, as it is independent of what is going on in the physical realm (John 14:27).

Isaiah 26:3 says, *"Thou wilt keep him in perfect peace, whose mind is stayed on thee, because he trusteth in thee."* Keep your thoughts and imaginations on Him, on the Word. When the enemy puts thoughts in your mind, don't breathe life into them by speaking them out loud. Never give voice to a lie. We are to take these thoughts captive. Don't entertain them. Replace a lie with the truth of God's Word by speaking what the Word says. When you speak it rather than thinking it, you are releasing your authority over that imagination and loosing angels on an assignment. Psalm 103:20 tells us that angels harken, they respond, and go into action at the voice of God's Word. Who gives God's Word voice? We do. The children of God. Release His Word, and angels go into action. Speak words in agreement with hell, and the demonic are acting on your words. Be careful what kingdom you are authorizing to act by your spoken words.

As an act of your will, you may need to make the quality decision to keep your mind and imagination in the proper perspective on a minute by minute or even second by second basis (Romans 12:2, 2 Corinthians 10:4-6). The battle is real. The enemy comes to us with thoughts. He wants these thoughts to eventually be planted into our heart so they will produce fruit of the antichrist spirit, and it takes your cooperation to do this, consciously or unconsciously (Proverbs 23:7). Choose not to come into agreement with thoughts that exalt themselves against the knowledge of Christ. For you to do this, you must know what the Word says. The Holy Spirit may give you a check in your spirit, too. Go search out the Word if you're unsure. The Holy Spirit is your Helper. He'll let you know when you're getting off track or if something is amiss. When He prompts you, heed that prompt immediately, without delay and make the necessary adjustments. The enemy is feeding fear to the masses with mainstream media's voice, for one. We're here to help eliminate that fear, not get caught up into it. Guard your gates.

Essential Components for the Church

The essential components of the end time Body of Christ are undeniably militant in nature. The Word of God tells us that we are more than conquerors (Romans 8:37). Conquerors use force. They subdue what needs to be brought down to the point where it is no longer able to function. Overpower, restrain, and defeat is what conquerors do. It's in their DNA, and they are absolutely sold out to their mission and utterly focused on their objective at all times. They know no fear and already see victory in their mind, imagining their triumph even before they begin to engage in battle. This is a powerful description of a conqueror, as well as a key to the power of our imagination. Keep in mind, we aren't battling with flesh and blood, with human beings. Ephesians 6:12 tells us our battle is with the unseen principalities and powers of the kingdom of darkness, wickedness in the spirit realm. This is part of having the right perspective, as well. We enforce the victory that Jesus died and shed His Blood to provide. He bought and paid for our victory. It's already done, and it's defined in the Word of God from Genesis to Revelation.

This aggressive, battle-ready, more than a conqueror mindset component is essential for every Believer. No one is exempt from engaging in disrupting the enemy's agenda. The importance of preparedness and being effectively ready for battle cannot be overemphasized. We will break down what this battle-ready component looks like in chapter four. It is important to keep this perspective in mind, though, as you read on. You are more than a conqueror, and we do battle in the heavenlies. We go to the root of the problem.

In essence, Roman 8:19 tells us that all creation is waiting on us to show the world Whose we are, who we are, and Who is in us. The Anointed One and His anointing has equipped us to take dominion over everything that steals, kills, and destroys, manifesting and demonstrating the Word of God by faith with the supernatural, thus revealing heaven's solutions. Miracles, signs, and wonders must follow us as Believers. Jesus is the answer to all of the hell that has been unleashed, and we are carriers of God and His glory. Essential, necessary and critical supernatural, miraculous components are required in this end time hour, and administered through us.

The Church IS Essential

The battle-ready Body of Christ, each one of us, is essential in establishing the Kingdom of God's governmental rule in every sphere of influence God has given us. This refers to every member, every part of the Body. As Christ's ambassadors, we speak on behalf of our King, imploring those who don't know God to come to Him. In each sphere we have influence, we co-labor with the Holy Spirit, bringing it back to a status that glorifies God; manifesting Whose we are, who we are, and Who is in us.

What a glorious time to be alive and doing our part to advance the Kingdom of God. I am so grateful to be a part of this end-time generation; the generation that is wrapping things up on earth before Jesus returns. Every local church member, and the Church globally, are essential in fulfilling the plan of God that He has ordained for the Church to do in this final hour. *"The earth shall be filled with the knowledge of the glory of the Lord as the waters cover the sea,"*

(Habakkuk 2:14) and the Lord is going to use us to see this prophetic, unstoppable Word manifest.

All creation has been waiting, and it is now time. It is our finest hour as we engage in the end time, strategic plan of God.

Chapter Two

Two Opposing Agendas

The line has been drawn. There is a distinction between good and evil that is so obvious right now. Unless someone's been hiding under a rock, as of March 2020, it's quite evident that the world is completely different than is has been since we've been born. Two diametrically opposing agendas, each with a very distinct and easily identifiable voice, are rallying troops at this very moment to strategically accomplish their mission at hand. The goal of each camp is clear, and the stakes are as high as they can get. It is law and order versus anarchy and lawlessness, life versus death, right versus wrong. We are seeing the intense conflict between the Kingdom of God and the kingdom of darkness. There is a turf war for our nation. Why? Because as America goes, so goes the world. But, as the Church goes, so goes America.

We are the only entity that has the authority and power to effectively deal with satan and his agenda. Man-made solutions cannot even come close to any viable solution. This evil must be addressed at the root, and it's in the realm of the spirit. What we see in the physical realm is indicative of the activity launched and continuing in the unseen.

Discernment

In Matthew 16:3 Jesus rebuked the Pharisees for not being able to discern or differentiate the signs of the times. Those who despised the Anointed One and His anointing were very well versed and had great understanding in forecasting natural events, i.e. storms; but these learned men were completely clueless when it came to discerning the signs of the times. They lacked spiritual discernment and were incapable of perceiving spiritual things. Natural signs they had down to a tee but were lost when it came to things of the spirit. Religion will do that to a person. Someone under the influence and bound by religion and/or the traditions of men is unable to recognize or comprehend spiritual things with the accuracy needed to bring about a Word-based resolution. This is not the example we are to follow. Jesus is our example, and we have the potential to operate with the same degree of discernment that He operated with.

Unfortunately, and dangerously so, today many in a five-fold ministry position or in any leadership capacity in the Church lack discernment. Deception and denial, or an unwillingness to allow the Word of God to be the final authority, run amuck in many churches in America as well as globally. This is one of the signs Jesus told His disciples we would see in the end times (Matthew 24:3-8). Many believers are, and will continue to be deceived, as a result of what is coming from many pulpits as well as a lack on their part of abiding in the vine (John 15:1-8). This absence or inadequate degree of insight could potentially result in a pandemic of ignorance that could bring destruction to the lives of countless Believers and the unsaved alike. God said His people are destroyed because they lack knowledge or have rejected it (Hosea 4:6). Ignorance is not bliss; it is extremely dangerous. We cannot afford to perpetuate ignorance, deception, or denial regarding the signs of the times. It could cost people their eternal salvation and God-given destinies.

This is a time where good versus evil is so obvious, yet many fail to recognize this indisputable scenario for what it truly is. Blinders are on the eyes of the lost, but on too many in the Church as well. It is a time when all hell has seemingly been unleashed. But, it is also the greatest hour for the Church, the Body of Christ. It is Christ in us, the anointing in and on us for this end time hour that will cause Habakkuk 2:14 to become tangible and undeniable. It's just what all creation is waiting for. The whole world is groaning with anticipation and calling for us to do something about the crisis humanity is facing. This is our hour to show off and display who our God is.

We are living in an hour where having spiritual discernment is critical. Without it, it is impossible to understand the nature of the beast that is attempting to silence the Church, destroy America - one nation under God, and control the masses globally. Sadly, many Believers don't have eyes to see or ears to hear the signs of the times or where are we in the scheme of things. It's important we understand what God wants and plans to do in this end time scenario. But it's also important we are not ignorant of the enemy's devices and what his agenda is, either (2 Corinthians 2:11).

There is a global attempt to silence the voice of God's people. The enemy is pulling out all the stops to silence the Church. He does not want the uncompromised Word preached, Believers gathered, or the standard of righteousness raised up against his tactical maneuvers. Satan knows his only hope is to stop our influence because we are the only entity on earth that has the authority to disrupt and confuse his operations and silence his voice. And there is no distance in the spirit realm. We can do severe damage to and halt his agenda even when it's not at a local level. Jesus said His Words are spirit and life (John 6:63). They are not confined to natural borders.

As the enemy coordinates efforts to establish the New World Order through people, governments, and systems, every Believer is needed to assume their position of influence in each role God directs them to step into. This deluge of evil must be confronted and subdued with prayer, with our God-given authority, and with the anointing of the Holy Spirit. God intends for the Church to rise up, mobilize, occupy individually and corporately, and be who we are designed to be – the most powerful entity on earth, and properly discern what is going on in the spirit.

Those in ministry have a responsibility to communicate to those they have influence over, with accuracy, the prophetic season we are living in and what we can do to thrive in these perilous times. We must stay completely void of all fear and operate with the peace that only Jesus can give us. Unless we have ears to hear clearly what God is telling us on how to navigate this time, we will fail to be on point and miss the mark. This is where the five-fold ministry comes in. It's up to us to teach, train, equip, and prepare those we feed with power-packed, nutrient-rich meals that will sustain a body in difficult and trying times. The Body needs spiritual food that is devoid of toxins or diluted to a state where there is no intrinsic value.

This is no time to be politically correct, people-pleasing, or passive. We have a responsibility to help folks grow up, teach them from the Word without watering it down, and train the saints to do the work of the ministry (Ephesians 4:12). There should be no players on the sidelines in these few final minutes of this game, no bench-sitting. Coaches, it's up to us to ensure each player gets in the game, be it rookie or pro. As the enemy coordinates efforts to establish one government and economic system through corrupt governments and systems, every Believer is needed to assume their position of influence well-trained, and engage with determination, boldness, confidence, courage, and most of all, with the anointing of the Holy Spirit.

The Assault on the Church

There is a war waging to silence and stop the Body of Christ from being the most influential, authoritative, dominant, and powerful force that it is designed and destined to be. These attempts to mute the voices of righteousness have never been more prevalent than they are now. Social media's frenzied and furious pursuits to silence and censor conservatives are fierce and yielding very disturbing results. Accounts are being blocked or even cancelled by the politically correct police, God-mockers that monitor social media platforms. Big tech giants use their overreaching power and influence, blacking out conservative verbiage, be it political or religious, as well as images that depict the stark contrast between good and evil or the lies from the truth. These companies are silencing those who raise up a standard that is contrary to their radical left, God-hating agenda.

The Body of Christ is a detrimental threat to satan's schedule of events which are fueled by the antichrist spirit working through these people in high places. The enemy's plan: establish the New World Order and usher in the antichrist. God's plan: Dominate every mountain of influence, advance the Kingdom of God, and prepare for the return of Jesus Christ.

Mainstream media, which is under the influence of a leviathan spirit, constantly twists and turns the facts, distorting the truths to the point they are completely unrecognizable. Data is manipulated to purposefully deceive their audience and victimize people with the purpose of stoking the flames of hostility and division. News is no longer news, but propaganda to reprogram the masses. The motive is clear - defame people who love Jesus, godly standards, and the United States of America. Instill hate and fear into the hearts of those who feed on these polluted food sources. Paint the picture that any voice countering their evil narrative is a bigot, hater, deplorable, and domestic enemy. This dross is perpetuated from key political figures in our nation, as well as corrupt business moguls that are hell-bent to destroy America and establish the New World Order. Driven by the love of money, greed for power, position, or control, they know no boundaries to the evil they are more than willing to operate in as they cooperate with satan.

Unethical, divisive, and nefarious politicians at every level in our nation and globally have deemed the Church "unessential." Doors to churches and religious gatherings have been closed, or allowed to open with a minimum seating capacity, strictly and intentionally limiting the size of the gatherings. More controls have been imposed with the intent to silence those who are authorized by God Himself to represent Him on earth. These people who walk in darkness see God and His children as indispensable and their voice needs to be eliminated. Singing in church, even while viewing online services, is prohibited by the governor of California. Pastors across the nation have received Cease and Desist orders from authorities that see no legitimacy to our first amendment because the Church is a threat to the destructive narrative hell is working hard to advance. Jail time and fines are used as threats to intimidate and manipulate Believers into submission.

The Church is rising up and refusing to be intimidated and silenced, no matter what threats are hurled towards it. All this despicable and vile deceit is under the guise of *it's for your own good because of a pandemic*. Those without spiritual discernment in this hour can easily fall victim to the antichrist spirit of deception, failing to see things as they really are, as well as where these tactics originate from. This end time evil that has been orchestrated by the enemy is intensifying, but he has overplayed his hand.

God is awakening His Church and we will not be intimidated, silenced, or succumb to fear. The stakes are too high. Not only are we standing up for our rights, that are clearly defined in our Constitution, but we have a world that has yet to be reached with the Gospel of the Kingdom. People need to be saved and set free from the darkness that has enslaved them.

Jesus is the only hope for this world. Christ is in us, and we carry the glory. This is our time to extend life-saving hands to everyone who is perishing while infiltrating enemy territory and operating with the anointing, co-laboring with the Holy Spirit to establish God's will. We are heaven's task force, armed and dangerous to all demonic efforts. None of us are here by accident. Like Esther, we are here for such a time as this. God has handpicked each one of us for this end time task force and has equipped us with all the arsenal we need to accomplish our mission with superb accuracy and emerge giving great glory to our God.

We fear nothing, we lack nothing, and we will stop at nothing. Our Commander and Chief, The Messiah, has instructed us to occupy until He comes for His Bride. Advance, take ground, rescue captives, and hold ground. *'On earth as it is in Heaven'* is our battle cry. We're here to take over, not take up space. We are essential to the thwarting of hell's advancements, rescuing captives, and producing miraculous solutions to problems across the globe.

Chapter Three

Our Responsibility

God is awakening the sleeping giant, His Church. As born again, Spirit-filled Believers, we must arise in response to this wake-up call, shake off the slumber, and get with Heaven's program. This is what each one of us must do, as well as help others wake up. Jesus appointed, authorized, and empowered us to occupy until He returns. A mandate such as this is not optional, elective, or discretional.

This dynamic, world-transforming call to action's purpose is to activate the Body of Christ like no other time in the history of mankind due to this critical and chaotic hour we are living in. Momentum of this Body will build an energy in the realm of the spirit, causing it to be a primary catalyst in our collective mobilization and successful occupation. The alarm is ringing. "Will I hit the snooze button intentionally? By reflex? Or will I allow the sound to resonate and provoke me enough to respond in accordance with Christ's directive?" This is something we all need to ask ourselves. Our individual and corporate response to this call must be congruent to the urgency of this hour.

It is time for the disengaged Believer or local church to awaken, shake off any slumber, arise, and be the most powerful, influential, and dominating force on planet earth as God Almighty intended us to be. We are to execute God's agenda in advancing His Kingdom.

This awakening will cause the truth of our purpose and identity to be realized and released to a greater degree, which in turn should propel us into immediate action causing us to discombobulate the spiritual darkness that has been controlling sectors of society far too long. Our identity is built on nothing less than Jesus Christ Himself in us, with us, and for us, which is the hope of planet earth being filled with the revelation and experiential knowledge of the glory of Jehovah God just as the waters cover the sea.

We must be good stewards of what has been entrusted to us as we prepare this place for the return of Jesus and disrupt and hold back the enemy's agenda of a One World Order. It is a glorious and honorable call on our lives. What a privilege it is to be assigned a part in God's end time, dominating, and reigning Church. The responsibility to acknowledge and obey our assignment rests in our will. God will not violate this free will He has endowed us with. We are not waiting on God, He is waiting on us to respond in faith and trust Him to work through us. See yourself as an instrumental part in His glory being unleashed wherever you are and release the anointing accordingly, in every sphere of influence as it is in heaven. Start at home and extend this anointing into the marketplace.

We have a serious problem in our midst though, which must be rectified immediately. Churches abound with Believers who aren't cognitive of their true identify, which is clearly defined in the Word of God. Who we are, Whose we are, what we are supposed to do, be, and possess is outlined from Genesis to Revelation. Biblical illiteracy and lack of know-how permeates much of the Body of Christ and is producing ineffective Body parts that have been purposed and empowered to see God's will manifest in every area of our lives and society. These Body parts are weak, lame, and incapable of productivity because of gross malnourishment. Instead of seeing miracles, signs, and wonders which are critically needed right now, we are witnessing massive fear, hopelessness, doubt, confusion, uncertainty, and victim mentality mindsets. LACK OF KNOWLEDGE has set the stage for these crippling agents from hell. God said in Hosea 4:6 that His people are broken, ruined, and destroyed because there is an absence or lack of insight, awareness, intelligence and/or they have denied, abandoned, and rejected knowledge, be it intellectual, experiential, or revelation.

In addition, a religious spirit empowers much of the Church to accommodate the dark agenda by disregarding selected Scriptures, encouraging leaders to create God in their own image, intentionally or ignorantly. This false god and idol that has been manufactured by flesh is then perpetuated throughout congregations and is evident by an environment that lacks any demonstration of the Word being preached. We've been mandated to rule and reign but need the nuts and bolts on how to walk this out responsibly and effectively.

The Responsibility of the Five-Fold Ministry

This inadequacy of knowledge can be traced back to a dominant root cause - church leadership. Apostles, prophets, evangelists, pastors, and teachers have been appointed by God to train, equip, and prepare the Body of Christ. It is time for the saints to be able to skillfully and effectively do the works of the ministry and bring a heavenly transformation across the globe, starting in our own communities. This equipping empowers the Church, each Body part, to be the

Church just like God intended it to be. It is to be the most powerful and influential force on this planet, taking charge, and taking ground. It is vital that we recognize the extent of this responsibility, its gravity, and the time we are living in as leaders. Then we MUST inform others and emphasize the importance of their cooperation with Heaven.

We have each been hand-picked by God Himself for such a critical time as this, fellow leaders. It is imperative that we are honest with ourselves and inspect the fruit that we are producing, using the Word of God as our mirror and being sensitive to the voice of the Holy Spirit. What adjustments are needed in our lives and ministries to best accommodate the One who has placed us in such a leadership position? Any leadership position is in reality a position of servanthood. How can we best serve others, so they in turn, can best serve others is a legitimate question to ask the Holy Spirit and ourselves on a daily basis.

Church leadership is either being led by the Holy Spirit, Who never contradicts Scripture, or by something other than the Spirit of God. The flesh, fear, incorrect perspectives, ignorance of the Word, and no anointing are all examples to consider. Any or all have the ability to cause someone to get off course by modifying Scripture to accommodate a belief, a mental stronghold, or a demonic influence. These alterations and adaptations are in reality, comfort zones that keep leadership from reaching the destination God has planned, not only for them, but for those under their influence.

If we stick to the unadulterated, undefiled Word of God and refuse to water down Scripture to make it more palatable, if we refuse to be led by man, the fear of man or any devil, if we are open to correction and allow the Holy Spirit to prune us so Genesis 1:28 becomes a hard copy in our lives, expect to make a major Godly impact in the spirit and physical realm alike. *"And God blessed them, and God said unto them, Be fruitful, and multiply, and replenish the earth, and subdue it: and have dominion over the fish of the sea, and over the fowl of the air, and over every living thing that moveth upon the earth,"* (Genesis 1:28). This command is a precise description of a Believer who is ruling, reigning, dominating in the spirit realm as evidenced in the physical realm. Using this as our litmus paper, so to speak, when self-evaluating, will provide us with an honest report. The Holy Spirit is such a great Teacher, Mentor, and Helper. Allow Him to do what He longs to do for you. Remain humble and teachable so He can help bring healthy transformation.

The reality of two agendas, as mentioned in chapter two, is undeniably heating up to higher degrees on a seemingly daily basis. The saints of God must be equipped properly to thrive in this hour, let alone survive. People that don't know God are waiting on us to reveal Who our God is if they know it or not. We *need* to thrive. This Love revealed, God revealed, will draw people to Jesus.

What hell has dispatched and continues to release is wreaking havoc in the lives of people. God loves people. It's up to us to instruct and impart what the Body needs to subdue satan's agenda. This takes the Word of God given out full-strength and uncompromised from whatever platform the Lord has given you. Meals like this will nourish and strengthen the Body's spiritual immune system to resist and ward off attacks from the enemy with a supernatural empowerment.

We must never allow picky eaters, those who like their ears tickled, to persuade us into adjusting what we teach and preach to satisfy their unhealthy appetites. Don't allow their flesh or your flesh to lead you. There are foundational teachings that must be the basis for what we deliver, and they will be addressed in the next chapter. We want to build strong Body parts, that are more than capable of producing evidence in their lives that they know their God. Great exploits should be a normal part of our lives as well as those we influence.

There is to be a very distinct line of demarcation, an undeniable difference between us and those who don't have a relationship with Christ. The world is searching for answers, remedies, and solutions that only we, as children of God, can provide. The lost want to know who to come to and where to go for the antidotes they are desperately searching for. Isaiah 8:18 says, *"Behold, I and the children whom the Lord hath given me are for signs and wonders in Israel from the lord of hosts, which dwelleth in mount Zion."* Signs, wonders, and miracles – miraculous solutions in every sphere of influence is Heaven's calling card.

It's time for all leaders who have been asleep and comforted by the status quo to respond in obedience to this wake-up call and shake off complacency with a vengeance. Then help others out of any spiritual stupor or lethargy they may be in. There is no time to waste. This is an extremely urgent wake-up call that must not be ignored. People's lives are at stake. We must not allow where they spend eternity be decided by the enemy. Jesus said in John 10:10, *"The thief cometh not, but for to steal, and to kill, and to destroy: I am come that they might have life, and that they might have it more abundantly."*

When we see something that represents satan's agenda, this is an extremely loud call to action, and we should do just that. Act. When we see people living lives less than what Jesus paid for with His Blood, this is also a call for our response. Equipping those we lead to defy evil and demonstrate the Kingdom of God is what we were born to do. The world needs well-equipped saints to put things in divine order. God wants His will done in earth. He works through His saints to bring the proper alignment needed that will cause His glory to be realized across the globe. This is our finest hour as leaders. See yourself and your giftings as essential, as fundamental. You are loaded, so let it loose!

The Responsibility of Every Believer

Each born-again Believer will respond in one way or another to this wake-up call. How each individual acknowledges this alarm will be evident by the words they speak or don't speak and by the actions they take or don't take. What is in the heart of every Believer will be revealed as a result. A self-assessment is critical in this hour. Each saint would benefit from taking a look at what fruit is being produced in their life initially and on a regular basis. Is there a misalignment in any area of life in view of what Scripture says? The Holy Spirit and Word of God will correct and readjust if we are willing. Wherever and whenever we are out of order and not allowing the Word of God to be the final authority, we miss God's best for us. Our response is at the mercy of our will. God cannot make us line up according to His end time agenda. We only need to be willing, submitting our will to His and obey.

Now is the time to allow God to do a greater work in us so He can do greater works through us. This transformation will come as a result of an abiding fellowship with the Holy Spirit, studying and meditating the Word and submitting to His leading. Obedience pays great dividends. Disobedience is very costly. Our lives and the lives of those who we are called to reach will be affected by our choices, either negatively or positively. Don't underestimate your part in the Body of Christ. You may be one person, but so was Mary, the mother of Jesus. In Luke 1:38 the angel released a word from Heaven and Mary responded in a way that would cooperate with God's agenda. The words this one young teenage girl spoke continue to reverberate from generation to generation. *"Be it unto me according to thy word,"* (Luke 1:38).

Mary submitted her will to God's will. There was a prophetic agenda that had to be fulfilled as spoken by the prophets. The time and location were detailed hundreds of years before the birth of Christ. It was time for the birth of Christ, the Messiah. This one person's response changed the trajectory of mankind's future and way of life in every sense possible. One *"Be it unto me according to your word"* was all it took to get the ball rolling that impacted the rest of mankind and all eternity. Our affirmative response to the call of God on us is just as important in His eyes.

All of Heaven responds to our words when they line up with the will of God. You may be one person, but there is more with you than be against you. When we declare, *"Be it unto me according to Your Word, Jesus,"* we are allowing the Word to take preeminence in our life. What the Bible says may not agree with a current belief or view we have, but when we stick with the Word, instead of something that is contrary to Scripture, we win. Your voice and actions in accordance to the Word are essential in bringing necessary transformation to the lives and destinies of yourself and others. You are here, right now, by God's design. He could have had you living a thousand years ago, but no. He chose you to be living now.

Everyone is responsible for what they allow into their ear and eye gate. *'Garbage in, garbage out'* is not a meaningless cliché, but a warning to heed. Pay attention to the choices you make. Who and what you listen to either promotes the agenda of heaven or hell.

Use these questions as an effective benchmark:

- Are you being equipped and strengthened by these influences in a way that enable you to advance the Kingdom of God?
- Is the Word of God being actualized in your life and the lives of those who speak into your life?
- Look at the fruit. What is being produced? What hardcopy evidence can you identify?
- Are you being challenged, built up, and encouraged out of any areas of passivity?
- Is the message from the pulpit a motivational or mobilization message?
- Is the Word of God being preached without any compromise or apology, untainted by the opinion of man and followed by demonstration?

- Are people being led to Jesus and baptized in the Holy Spirit?

Honestly evaluate your answers and ask God to direct you to the local church He wants you to plug into so you can fulfill what He has called you to do as well as be a blessing to that local church. You may have already been feeling a prompting or gut-instinct that something was amiss. Don't disregard that nudge. Whatever He tells you to do, obey. Do not allow manipulation, guilt, or pressure from anyone taint your decision.

The enemy is a deceiver and can present something to you that sounds and looks very spiritual, but it is designed with the intent to steal, kill, and destroy your abundant life and effectiveness. There is an epidemic of watering down the Word of God and rewriting Scripture to accommodate the spirit of the age. Religion will produce a gross misrepresentation of God. If you don't know the what the Bible says about any given situation or topic, warning! You are a prime candidate for deception. It's time to grow up.

We must not depend on those who teach and preach as our only source of spiritual nourishment but take responsibility and feed ourselves. Study God's Word. Fellowship and commune with Jesus regularly. Be sensitive to the promptings of the Holy Spirit. Jesus warned the disciples that deception, even among those in leadership, would be a sign of His soon coming. It is imperative that we develop ears to hear what the Holy Spirit is saying and be quick to obey. Do not fellowship with deception, no matter what form it comes in.

Messages and teachings that appease the flesh, feel good, and cause us to be weak in the things of God are dangerous. Motivational and entertaining messages will not suffice in this hour. The devil is hell bent on establishing a global world order and destroying people. Understanding the role you have in promoting and establishing God's Kingdom agenda right now is imperative. Allow the Word to have the last say in your life, rather than a belief, doctrine, or teaching that is contrary to what Scripture says. You won't go wrong when you agree with the Word. You'll get flack from some, but you are choosing life. Take the flack and get on with what God has for you. He'll help you no matter what comes against you. Your strength is in Him (Psalm 118:14, Joel 3:10, Ephesians 6:10).

The enemy knows, without a shadow of a doubt, once a Believer starts operating in accordance to their true identity and sees how essential they are to Heaven's agenda, they immediately become a detrimental threat to his plans and purposes. Hell's agenda is in grave danger when a Believer has a revelation of and unleashes Christ and His anointing in them. Jesus destroyed the works of the enemy (1 John 3:8). It is our responsibility to enforce this victory everywhere we set foot, including in our own homes. Walk in the authority you have as a Believer and release that authority with your faith-filled words (Matthew 8:5-13). Remember, we are mandated to occupy until Jesus returns and His return is sooner than most realize.

There is an all-out demonic assault on the Body to keep every saint and local church in a state of ignorance, including five-fold leaders and lay people. Not knowing the Word on an intimate basis in any given area of life causes the Body of Christ to remain ineffective and unproductive in advancing the Kingdom of God. This is an unacceptable state of existence for any local church or Believer, especially as we rapidly approach the end of this era.

The Kingdom of God has provided us with everything needed to be the unconquerable force that cannot be overcome by hell's attempts because we are already positioned and seated in the place of victory. We are the

Church of Jesus Christ. We are essential in dismantling systems that promote and empower the devil's agenda and replace darkness with the *manifested* Word of God. People don't need to hear just another sermon or attend one more Bible study without any manifestation of the Word becoming flesh or an undeniable manifestation of the miraculous. It is imperative they not only *hear* the Kingdom of God taught and preached but experience a DEMONSTRATION of the power of the Holy Spirit and the Word confirmed with supernatural signs and wonders. Period. This should be a normal occurrence and it will be when we allow the Holy Spirit to do what He does. Tragically, the simplicity of this is very often distorted by religion and unbelief. It's the demonstration of the Gospel that is irrefutable evidence that our glorious Jesus is alive. The world must know that He is undeniably alive. They must experience Jesus.

Without us responding to this wake-up call, the world remains in a hopeless state. The devil knows his time is short. This is indeed the greatest hour for each member of the Body of Christ to come out of the closet and co-labor with the Spirit of God to demonstrate Who our God is and how much He loves humanity. The enemy has no shortage of representatives. It is essential for the Church to accurately represent the love and power of a God that died for us and lives in us.

Chapter Four

Back to Basics

It is vitally important that each member of the Body of Christ be rooted and grounded in the basics given to us in Scripture to live and operate by faith. These foundational teachings are essential for every Believer to live an unlimited, victorious life here on earth, no matter what obstacles and persecution come into play. These are prerequisites for our healthy spiritual growth and development. Without laying a solid foundation in the beginning of the construction process, it would be futile to build a structure and expect it to maintain its integrity for any length of time. Storms comes in multiple forms. Once faced with any type of adversity or agitation, the structure is potentially compromised, depending on the strength and duration of whatever is battering the structure. Detrimental effects produced by the elements may not be noticeable immediately. Some may go undetected for years, but yet, they exist.

Parallel this example to a Believer's life. Without the proper elementary teachings required in laying a solid foundation for advanced instruction, growth, and maturity, we are not doing ourselves or anyone else any favors. This violent clashing of good versus evil will intensify. It is imperative we know how to stand strong and not bow to false ideologies, dead gods, or any sort of pressure. We can't afford to be weak and lame when we have a race to run and to run without looking back.

God predestined us to live in this end time. We have a great work to do in holding back and disrupting the plans of the enemy. As he attempts to establish a global government and economic system, by working through corrupt people, remember this: GOD has a plan for this end time as well. It is to establish His Kingdom on earth, and He will do it through His Body, the Church of Jesus Christ. He will do it through you.

What this world needs are strong, mature Believers who know their God, know who they are in Christ, and know how to operate Kingdom principles and spiritual laws, working in tandem with the Holy Spirit to establish the Father's will in earth. God warns us about ignorance in Hosea 4:6. Lack of or rejection of knowledge is detrimental to the spiritual health of any Believer and is certain to be revealed in their physical world and everyday life. Back to basics is needed now more than ever as the Church continues to awaken, arise, and assume its proper position in this hour. Back to basics is what new souls coming into the Kingdom will need to grow and remain strong no matter what adversity they may face.

Establishing a rock-solid groundwork for continued advancement, success, and productivity in the life of a Believer may differ somewhat from church to church, or from Bible study to Bible study. But the basics must not be compromised in any way, shape, or form. We must never allow the Message to be altered to accommodate man.

The Bible gives us the essentials needed to live a victorious, successful, and productive life now. We are not called to survive, but to thrive and live a life of complete victory in every area of life, no matter what is going on in the world. This life must be defined by the Word of God and not subject to the opinion of man, to dead religious beliefs, or in cooperation with an antichrist spirit that has infiltrated the globe. Stick with the Word of God and you will have Word of God results. When Jesus said in John 10:10, *"The thief cometh not, but for to steal, and to kill, and to destroy: I am come that they might have life, and that they might have it more abundantly,"* He meant what He said. Jesus didn't add an addendum that stated, *"unless it's the final hour and the antichrist spirit is attempting to establish a global world order."* God's Word is eternal. He knew the literal hell we'd be facing now. He still stands by His original declaration.

God said, *"For the earth shall be filled with the knowledge of the glory of the Lord, as the waters cover the sea,"* in Habakkuk 2:14. This prophetic declaration will soon become a tangible reality, one that our five physical senses will be unable to deny. Nations will have an undeniable move of God ranging from the north, south, east, and west. This is a global move of God, not just a few geographical locations or Holy Ghost hot spots.

God is faithful. It is impossible for Him to lie. Isaiah 46:11 says, *"I have spoken it, I will also bring it to pass. I have purposed it, I will also do it."* Make no mistake about it. God will bring this to pass, but it is our responsibility, as His Body, to cooperate with Him and be prepared to do, not only what He says to do, but how and when to do it. Getting back to the basics, as laid out in the Word of God, will equip and produce people that truly know God. As a result, they can expect to do great and miraculous exploits that will glorify God. This is what will distinguish us from the rest of the world. The lost, anyone without hope, people serving dead gods, will come face to face with the love of the Father and given an opportunity to give their lives to Christ.

The foundational teachings, designed to establish us as a force to be reckoned with, as simple as they are, they are the most dominant principles that can effectively unseat and eradicate anything that exalts itself against the will of God. Be prepared. God is about to do something so glorious and unlike anything the world has ever seen or experienced before (Exodus 34:10, Isaiah 43:19). This is the Church's finest hour as we are about to see the line of demarcation between us and the world's failing systems so distinct that it will be impossible to deny this is the Lord's doing and it's marvelous and unmatched in our sight.

Satan's evil and quickly disintegrating structures are collapsing. Everything he touches dies. These systems, as defined and fueled by the demonic, are crying out for the righteous to assume positions of influence that will be instrumental in the glory of God covering the earth. Family, government, religion, education, business, media, arts, and entertainment are all in dire need of a Blood transfusion, and we're just the generation to help the Holy Spirit in unleashing the greatest move of God mankind has ever experienced. Get ready to see and be used by heaven to do the miraculous like never before.

Basics can be boiled down to priorities. There is a divine and holy order we are to adhere to. The Word of God defines the proper order and sequence we are to consider on a daily basis, ensuring nothing encroaches on this order. Basics of all basics is as follows: God first, family second, followed by ministry, business, and so on. If we fail to keep these in proper alignment, everything else will be disjointed. If something is out of position in our body, we may feel physical pain as a result. Once there has been an adjustment made and order restored, the body can heal and pain resolve. Any disorder in our lives that contradict the divine order God has established will open wide the door to pain, adversity, and distress. Strife, division, unforgiveness, and offense will be lurking in the darkness, just waiting for an opportunity to reveal their destructive and venomous nature, making their presence known in relationships with the ones we are closest to.

Because of the critical hour we are living in, the tendency for some may be to put ministry before family and exert an enormous amount of effort and energy into the Kingdom work at hand. We must not confuse working our assignment with putting God first place in our life and growing in intimacy with Him. Our relationship with Jesus must be solid and that takes spending quality time with Him. The enemy would like to keep us so busy that precious relationships weaken, suffer, and are even destroyed at the cost of being 'busy for Jesus'. The devil is determined to destroy families, as solid marriages and families are the bedrock of society. Pornography, divorce, drugs, alcohol, and suicide are all too familiar in the world, as well as in the Church. Keeping our priorities in proper order will help guard and protect our lives, our homes, and our future. Be the Church in our homes first, then extend out from there.

Teach and mentor others regarding the importance of this order and placement. Then continue to lay the foundation needed for a *'more than a conqueror'* life needed to courageously and authoritatively take on the adversities that confront us. We cannot do this in our own strength, though. Collaborating with the Holy Spirit and yielding to His direction and leading is mandatory. His system and ways of doing and being are designed for our success. We've all been programmed with a system that has been designed and orchestrated for failure. These old ways of thinking and doing are counterproductive and cannot mix with the system of God. You are in the world but not of the world (John 15:19, 17:14-16). You're either all in or all out. No longer are we to allow our senses, our reasoning, or our will to direct us. This is guaranteed failure. If we choose to make our life about Him and not about us, we're going to come out on top.

The following list consists of basic teachings, foundational basics which are all about Him, and needed in the life of every Believer. There are other basics to take into consideration, but these are 'front burner' and must not be omitted. It's always beneficial to go back to the basics. These fundamental building blocks support who we are, what we can do, and what we possess. Get these down into your heart. Teach and build others up in these areas.

The basics have been lacking in the Church, but this is a new day. When you get a revelation of the basics, you can't HELP but wake up and get with the program. You'll be more than ready to run to any problem and bring the Jesus solution. All of Heaven is backing you up, and you have the Holy Spirit and angels assisting you at every angle. If you find you are lacking any teaching or understanding in any of these areas, it is important for you to find a Word-filled, faith-filled, Holy Spirit-filled person or ministry to help you out.

This list of basics paints a clear picture of the elements of a battle-ready, more than a conqueror Believer. Having knowledge and an understanding of these basics is vitally important. Even when it comes down to a life or death situation, you'll be more than ready to handle it as you work in tandem with the Holy Spirit. You don't need to be an expert to employ this arsenal. Knowing what you have in your hand is a great advantage, then build on that knowledge and gain understanding by listening to anointed teachers and by use. Don't be afraid to start where you're at.

Our Fundamental Basics/Essentials

- The Word of God
    - Must be our final authority in every situation, in every area of life because it alone is the Truth. *(Psalm 119:151,160, John 17:17, 2 Timothy 3:16, 1 Peter 1:23)*
    - **Jesus is the Word.** *(John 1:1-5,14, Revelation 19:13)*
    - It is eternal and immutable. *(Psalm 119:89,160, Isaiah 40:8, 1 Peter 1:25).*
    - He is the same yesterday, today, and forever. *(Hebrew 13:8)*

- Salvation *(John 3:16, 14:6, 1 John 2:2, 4:14)* and Lordship of Jesus *(Philippians 2:5-11, Luke 6:46-49)*
  - Redemption *(Galatians 3:13-14, Ephesians 1:7, Titus 2:14)*
  - Righteous and a new identity – a new creation in Christ *(Genesis 1:26, 2 Corinthians 5:17, Galatians 2:20)*
- Water baptism
  - Public show of repentance and now a Believer *(Acts 19:4, Matthew 28:19-20)*
  - Supernatural power of water baptism, opens up an unseen realm *(Mark 1:9-11)*
- The Baptism of the Holy Spirit is not an option *(Matthew 3:13-17, Acts 1:4-8, 2:1-47)*
  - What the anointing is, what it does, how to release it for miracles, signs and wonders *(Isaiah 61:1-3, Acts 10:38, James 5:14, 1 John 2:20)*
  - Great Commission *(Mark 16:15-20)*
    - Know how to lead others to Christ and pray for them to receive the baptism of the Holy Spirit *(John 3:16, Romans 10:9-10, Acts 1:8)*
    - Heal the sick, cast out devils, raise the dead, make disciples. The supernatural is

bait for the unbeliever. *(Matthew 10:7-8, 28:19)*

- The Name of Jesus *(Acts 4:12,30, Romans 10:13, Philippians 2:9-11)*
- Communion and the Power of the Blood of Jesus. The supernatural power of taking communion *(Mark 14:22-24, 1 John 1:7, Revelation 12:11)*
- Finished works of Jesus *(2 Peter 1:3-4, Galatians 3:13)*
- Faith *(Romans 4:13-22, 2 Corinthians 5:7, Hebrews 11, 12:1-2)*
- Kingdom of God *(Luke 17:20-21, Romans 14:17, 1 Corinthians 4:20)*
- The Blood Covenant *(Hebrews 8:7-13, 10:16-23)*
- Tithing, sowing, reaping – prosperity *(Psalm 35:27, Malachi 3:8-12, 2 Corinthians 9:6-11)*
- Prayer and fasting *(Ezekiel 22:30, Mark 11:24-25, 1 John 5:14-15, Jude 1:20, Matthew 6:16-18)*
- Authority of the Believer *(Luke 10:19, Ephesians 1:19-23, James 4:7)*
- The armor of God *(Ephesians 6:10-18)*
- The power of our words *(Job 22:28, Proverbs 18:21, Mark 11:12-24)*
- Angels *(2 Kings 6:16, Psalm 91:11, 103:20, Hebrews 1:14)*

- Meditate the on the Word of God *(Joshua 1:8, Psalm 1: 1-3, 119:15-16)*
    - Revelation knowledge *(Psalm 119:18, Ephesians 1:17-20, Colossians 1:9-12)*
    - Renew your mind *(Proverbs 23:7, Romans 12:2)*

It's extremely helpful when studying the Word to refer to different versions of the Bible. When doing this, you can get a greater degree of understanding and revelation. When the Holy Spirit highlights a particular word to you, study it out. Dig into other Scriptures that have the same word. Even look up the word He emphasizes in a thesaurus and dictionary. You'll be surprised at how much will be revealed to you when you make an extra effort. It is quite an adventure when you dig deep into the Word of God by doing these simple things. You will sense faith rising up in your spirit, along with a supernatural boldness and confidence.

Chapter Five

The Winning Attitude

One of my favorite accounts in the Bible is found in the thirteenth and fourteenth chapters of Numbers. It represents an accurate picture of where we are today in many respects. God instructed Moses to send 12 spies out on a reconnaissance mission. Their instructions were clear. Courageously go into Canaan, the land God was giving to the children of Israel. Gather information by visual observation. Conduct a survey of this land and return with a full report on the number and condition of the inhabitants thereof. Assess the quality of the land and produce. Bring back crop samples of the fruit growing in that region.

These 12 spies went out as ordered and conducted their mission, returning with fresh fruit and verbal reports on the land and the inhabitants. Reporting to Moses, Aaron, and the children of Israel, this is a synopsis of the information provided. *The land was fertile, producing grapes so large that it took two men to carry one cluster of grapes suspended on a pole. The fruit was shown as evidence of what the land was capable of producing. This land was loaded with goods.*

The cities were reinforced and large and so were its inhabitants.

Here is what we need to zero in on. The 12 leaders were all in agreement that the land was exceptional. It was not like anything they had ever experienced in their lifetime. Yet, they were not in agreement with the most important aspect of all. The majority of the spies were convinced they were not able to take the land. Out of the abundance of the heart, the mouth speaks. The excuses were rolling off their tongues second nature. Based on the words they released, possessing any such land was out of the question. Only Joshua and Caleb were fully persuaded that they could take this land in spite of any obstacle. Not only take the land but do so immediately. These two didn't factor a waiting period into the equation, either. They quieted down the riotous mob and boldly proclaimed that they were more than able to take this land and dominate it without delay. The other 10 leaders interjected an ill-perceived image of themselves, along with the negative *'no can do, let's call it quits,' because these giants are intimidating and we're like grasshoppers in comparison'* report.

All 12 leaders saw the exact same thing when they surveyed the land and processed the information gathered by their five physical senses. Yet, two conflicting reports were conveyed to Moses, Aaron, and the masses. The majority of leaders released a defeated, hopeless word to the people. They were convinced that they didn't have what it took to do the job God had appointed them to do. This is the corrupt message they conveyed to their people. Joshua and Caleb had a resolve that the other leaders lacked. They were of a different spirit. Refusing to be denied of what God had planned for them, they saw and said this land of abundance was there for the taking. They were speaking just like God and paid no heed to the opposing voices and obvious resistance.

These two mighty men of valor, as an act of their own free will, chose not to rebel against God nor to fear the giants and in turn, released a life-giving report. The assessment Joshua and Caleb provided was in agreement with God's agenda. Their words echoed God's words. This good news was not well received by the people by any means, though. The children of Israel, God's own people, as an act of *their* will chose to side with the negative message preached by their 10 pastors. They saw themselves as their leaders saw themselves: unable to do what God has called them to do, inadequate, and weak. What was possible according to God, was deemed impossible by these 10 spies. Being led by fear and intimidation, not seeing themselves as God saw them, and speaking words designed by hell to stifle the plan of God, ignited a response from the people that was fueled by their leaders' rejection of the truth.

The congregation wanted to kill the two who preached the Word of God. Standing up for what was right was not well-received by everyone, just as it isn't today. Persecution is no stranger to the Church, to those who stand boldly and courageously for God's standard and His agenda, even within the Church. Persecution will continue to escalate as the time of Jesus' return draws nearer and nearer. This is not to cause us to fear, but it's a word to be prepared. God is with us and we have absolutely no cause to fear. God never gives us permission to fear, and we really have no right to fear as citizens of the Kingdom of God.

Here is my point. Joshua and Caleb possessed and displayed a winning attitude, determination, and commitment. The evidence of this was obvious by the words coming out of their mouths. There was an authority released when they spoke faith-filled words in agreement with God's plan and purpose. These words were containers of faith, of conquering, possessing, and taking over a land that was unfamiliar to them. They had already seen this mandate from God done in their heart. They imagined it as possible. Opposition and resistance were sure things, but so was the manifestation of the assignment, if they obeyed God. The mighty men of God wouldn't allow the voice of the enemy to take up real estate in their head and forbid any imagination that was contrary to their calling to displace the victory they already possessed in their heart. They refused to focus, magnify, and come into agreement with any lie. They wouldn't be held captive by any comfort zone that may have had influence over them in the past.

God had shown Himself faithful to the children of Israel, performing signs that were undeniably the Lord's doing. He had shown Himself trustworthy and not a man that He would lie. Still, 10 out of 12 leaders preached a defeated sermon which was incapable of producing any motive for movement or faith in the congregation to act on God's directive. But Joshua and Caleb knew their God, and that intimate knowing could not be matched, nor extinguished by the forces of darkness. Rather than seeing themselves as possible victims, they saw themselves as the victors, ready to do great exploits that would glorify Jehovah God.

How does this tie into what we are here for today? Remember, God appointed us to live during this end time era. He didn't want us living at any other time, just as He chose Joshua and Caleb to live in the generation they were living. It's important we see the significance of divine placement and how, in the words of Joshua and Caleb, we are well able to do what God has called us to do, to possess, and to be. Our role and cooperation with God's agenda have a degree of significance that cannot be measured by human standards, all with the sole purpose of advancing the Kingdom of God on planet earth and stopping hell.

This is a critical hour for all humanity, and we are here as ambassadors of Christ to establish the government of His Kingdom. Like Joshua and Caleb, it is paramount we are of a different spirit than those who don't know their God. Great exploits, solutions, answers to problems in every area of life are what we are here to deliver. We are well able, and we must act without delay.

A major deciding factor that will determine if we will effectively engage in this end time scenario and be the Church, will be this - who are we listening to? The vast majority of the preachers that returned from Canaan perpetuated the lie that fulfilling Heaven's assignment on their lives was an impossibility. In their own strength, it was. They had their eyes on themselves instead of on God. Our focus is so important.

What God had told them to do was just not going to happen, they were going to have no part of it and may as well go back to Egypt. At least in Egypt, they were familiar with that land and knew what to expect. Life in Egypt, even though it was a brutal existence, was still better in their eyes than facing giants in a quest to conquer a land that was inhabited by gigantic intimidating demonic beings. Fear of new territory, going and doing things that they had never done before, was not palatable to those who wouldn't obey or believe God. Same goes for today. The congregation was defeated in their own sight, even before they attempted to do anything or make an effort to possess the promised land. Based on what was coming from the pulpit, because of a misrepresentation of the Word, the occupation of Canaan by God's own people was incomprehensible and inconceivable in their eyes.

Joshua and Caleb acted on the Word of God. They preached the Word of God – WE ARE WELL ABLE TO POSSESS THE LAND. This is the message that we need coming from Church leadership now more than ever. The winning attitude must be one that permeates the Church. Each individual

Believer must have this mindset and heart belief to thrive in this hour. We are more than conquerors. This is our true identity. We are not grasshoppers. Any message that promotes an ideal that cannot be verified by Scripture must be eliminated from our spiritual diet. No exceptions, no arguments, and no delay.

Attitude is a major factor in determining how far anyone will go. We are each responsible for our own attitudes and can no longer blame someone else or any situation for a poor attitude. Attitudes will be challenged greatly in this hour as the onslaughts against the Church by those who hate and mock God. Remember our battle is not against flesh and blood. Let's learn a valuable lesson from the account in Numbers. What can we personally do to ensure our attitude is one that reflects who we are? What can we do to help others make the proper attitude adjustments? This is a great time to make the necessary modifications to accommodate nothing less than a countenance that causes us to stand out in a world that is under the sway of satan.

We are commissioned to go into unfamiliar territory and possess the land, just as the 12 leaders were called to possess Canaan. What is occurring in our nation and around the world now is an experience we've never faced before. We are facing giants that can be extremely intimidating and fearful. They are igniting an attitude of defeat and hopelessness for multitudes. Tragically, many Believers are stumbling around as in the dark, confused and dazed by the upheaval of what was once considered normal, just as the lost are. The Church must maintain an attitude that reflects Who our God truly is.

The *can do* attitude displayed by Joshua and Caleb, the demeanor that insists we are able because of Christ in us, the hope of glory, is a powerful magnet. This magnet is pulling those who are desperate for answers and solutions that the world undoubtedly cannot provide, towards the light and life of the Living God. It's getting darker and darker out there, but it's also our finest hour as the Church. The glory of God will be demonstrated on a grand scale, making us clearly distinguishable from the world. A light that no gross darkness can even come close to extinguishing. The earth WILL be filled with the knowledge of God's glory just as sure as waters fill the sea. God released this Word through the prophet Habakkuk, and He will hasten to perform His Word. The Church is essential. Anyone who declares otherwise is treading on extremely dangerous ground. Jesus is Lord, and soon coming King. We can do this Church! We are MORE than able to do every single thing that needs to be done, as directed by the Holy Spirit. Let's go up at once and be the dominating force on this planet that God has designed and empowered us to be. This truly IS our greatest hour, and we are essential!

Receive Jesus as Your Savior

God loves you! This love He has for you is unconditional. It makes no difference to Him what you may have done in the past or possibly still doing today. There is nothing that you could even imagine doing that has the ability to separate you from His love. John 3:16 tells us that the Father loved us, the world, so much that He sent Jesus to die for our sins. He shed His precious and powerful Blood so we could be cleansed from every sin. Jesus died on the cross for you. He also rose from the dead and is alive today. God wants you to spend eternity with Him, instead of in hell, and give you a victorious life here on earth. Romans 10:9-10,13 tells us that if we believe this in our heart and call upon the Name of Jesus, we can be assured of our salvation. Now is the right time to receive Jesus as your Savior. Don't wait one more moment or keep Him waiting any longer. He's there with open arms.

Pray this out loud:
Father, I believe Jesus died for my sins and was raised from the dead. Jesus, I confess You as my Savior and Lord. Jesus, I ask You to come into my heart. Thank You for saving me. Help me to live for You all the days of my life.

The Baptism of the Holy Spirit

We all need supernatural power to live the life God wants us to experience and fulfill our destiny. Since you are now His child, you can receive this empowerment from Him. You simply need to ask, believe, and receive what He has for you (Luke 11:9-13).

Pray this out loud:

Lord, fill me with Your Holy Spirit with the evidence of speaking in my heavenly prayer language. Thank You for this supernatural power. In Jesus' Name, amen.

About the Author:

Sue Foster is passionate about equipping the Body of Christ to boldly engage in the Great Commission by teaching Believers how to overcome comfort zones and expect the supernatural to be normal in their lives. Sue has been involved in ministry for over 40 years. She is a graduate of Victory Bible College in Tulsa, OK and the Joseph Business School in Forest Park, IL. Originally from Madison, WI, Sue and her husband, Jim, currently reside in Grand Rapids, MI.

To contact Sue, please write or email:

PO Box 364, Comstock Park, MI 49321
Website: www.suefoster1.com
Email: sue@suefoster1.com

Books by Sue Foster are available at
www.nationofwomenpublishing.com
Including, soon to be released,
"How to Get Out of Your Comfort Zone"

The Church Essential